Encouraging Thoughts for Women

Blessings

Written and compiled by MariLee Parrish.

Print ISBN 978-1-68322-213-2

Published by Barbour Books, an imprint of Barbour Publishing, Inc., P.O. Box 719, Uhrichsville, Ohio 44683, www.barbourbooks.com

Our mission is to publish and distribute inspirational products offering exceptional value and biblical encouragement to the masses.

Printed in the United States of America.

Encouraging Thoughts
for Women
———
Blessings

BARBOUR BOOKS
An Imprint of Barbour Publishing, Inc

Contents

Introduction

Return to your rest, my soul, for the LORD
has been good to you. For you, LORD,
have delivered me from death, my eyes
from tears, my feet from stumbling.
PSALM 116:7–8 NIV

———————

Has God been good to you? If you are going through a rough time, you may have a hard time answering that question! Go to God in prayer and ask Him to bring to mind all of the ways He has blessed you throughout your lifetime. You may be surprised as He reveals His hand throughout your life—burdens He has turned into blessings, disappointments He has turned into answered prayer, and ashes He has turned into beauty. Return to your rest, dear one, for God really has been good to you! He has brought you out of darkness and into His marvelous light (1 Peter 2:9). Enjoy the truths you find in these pages as a beautiful and amazingly loved child of God!

FRESH
START

Pick Up
the Blessings

"Repent therefore, and turn back,
that your sins may be blotted out,
that times of refreshing may come
from the presence of the Lord,
and that he may send the Christ
appointed for you, Jesus."
ACTS 3:19-20 ESV

Is your life at peace with God, or do you often feel stressed and far from your Creator? Do you feel overburdened and underrefreshed? Our fast-paced lifestyles often leave little room for the blessings of God. We load our schedule with good things, but maybe some of those good things take away from God's best. If you are having trouble hearing from God, it's time for a fresh start! This scripture in Acts tells us to begin with repentance. Quiet yourself before God and ask Him to search your heart (Psalm 139:23-24), to show you anything in your life that is not of God. Confess anything that God brings to mind, and ask Him for the power to turn from these sins. Talk to God about the busyness of your life. Ask Him for help creating room in your life to hear the voice of the Holy Spirit. Commit yourself to a fresh start in Christ so that times of refreshing can come from the presence of God in your life.

As the Spirit of God speaks to you, lay down your burdens—not on another person but on Jesus Himself—and pick up the blessings He offers you as you turn to Him moment by moment.

There is therefore now no condemnation
for those who are in Christ Jesus.
ROMANS 8:1 ESV

My dear children, I write this to you so
that you will not sin. But if anybody does sin,
we have an advocate with the Father—
Jesus Christ, the Righteous One.
1 JOHN 2:1 NIV

"Remember not the former things,
nor consider the things of old.
Behold, I am doing a new thing;
now it springs forth, do you not
perceive it? I will make a way in the
wilderness and rivers in the desert."
ISAIAH 43:18-19 ESV

There are far, far better things
ahead than any we leave behind.
C. S. LEWIS

———————

Anything can happen if you let it.
MARY POPPINS

———————

For last year's words
belong to last year's language
And next year's words
await another voice.
And to make an end
is to make a beginning.
T. S. ELIOT

Fresh Start

*"I will give you a new heart
and put a new spirit within you."*
EZEKIEL 36:26 NKJV

Some of the most surprising news about God's presence is that He does more than fix you up the best He can and send you on your way—somehow He makes you brand-new. His offer of new life is one of the few truly fresh starts you can experience. Sure, He doesn't delete the consequences that still have to be battled through, but He does have the power to change your heart and help you manage those consequences. Ask Him to make you new!

Renew My Heart

Father God, I come to You to renew my heart.
Show me anything in my life that is not from
You. I only want what You have for me, Father.
Fill me with Your presence and Your peace as
I bring all of my thoughts and worries to You.
Open my ears to hear Your voice and know
that it's You. Guide me as I walk in Your
truth. In Jesus' name, amen.

*And we know that for those who
love God all things work together
for good, for those who are
called according to his purpose.*
ROMANS 8:28 ESV

"For I know the plans I have for you,"
declares the LORD, *"plans to prosper
you and not to harm you, plans to
give you hope and a future."*
JEREMIAH 29:11 NIV

"A thief is only there to steal and kill
and destroy. I [Jesus] came so they can
have real and eternal life, more and
better life than they ever dreamed of."
JOHN 10:10 MSG

———————

"He will wipe away every tear from their eyes,
and death shall be no more, neither shall there
be mourning, nor crying, nor pain anymore,
for the former things have passed away."
REVELATION 21:4 ESV

Start Living It

Once made perfect, [Christ] became the source
of eternal salvation for all who obey him.
HEBREWS 5:9 NIV

You truly are the perfect woman. Others may bring up
your past or point out your mistakes, but God has made
you perfect through His Son, Christ Jesus. Your old life is
passed away and all things are new. You have a fresh
start—a clean slate. God doesn't remember the old you.
Every sin has been forgotten in His mind. Forget it in
yours. It's a new day with new dreams. You have been
given a whole new life. Start living it!

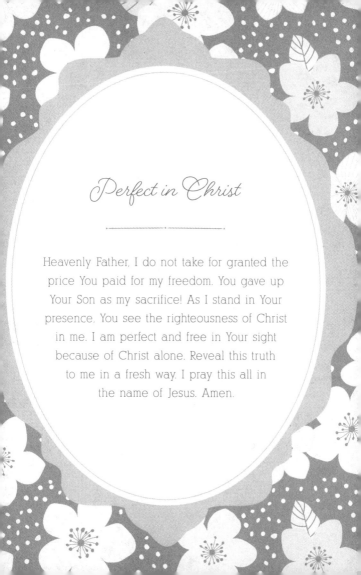

Perfect in Christ

Heavenly Father, I do not take for granted the price You paid for my freedom. You gave up Your Son as my sacrifice! As I stand in Your presence, You see the righteousness of Christ in me. I am perfect and free in Your sight because of Christ alone. Reveal this truth to me in a fresh way. I pray this all in the name of Jesus. Amen.

Let us fly from the Past
on the wings of Faith.
JAMES LENDALL BASFORD

You must learn, you must let God
teach you, that the only way to get
rid of your past is to make a future
out of it. God will waste nothing.
PHILLIPS BROOKS

Start by doing what's necessary;
then do what's possible; and suddenly
you are doing the impossible.
FRANCIS OF ASSISI

PRESENCE
OF GOD

Day by Day

---

*You make known to me the path of life;
you will fill me with joy in your presence,
with eternal pleasures at your right hand.*

PSALM 16:11 NIV

Life seems to be a great mystery. What is our purpose here? What is happening in our mixed-up world? We are the children of the living God, and He makes His ways known to us little by little, day by day, moment by moment. As we seek Him and learn to hear His voice, He fills us with joy even in the darkest times. Sometimes this joy and peace don't even make sense (Philippians 4:6-7)! When everyone in our lives says we should feel or act or be a certain way because of our circumstances, Jesus says, "Come to Me and I will tell you who you really are and what I'm doing with your life."

The presence of God in our lives changes everything! He is with us. He is closer than you might think. The Spirit of the living God lives in us! And He is willing and able to meet every one of your needs. Needs you don't even know you have. All He wants from you is to "come" (Matthew 11:28-30). Everything else will fall into place as you rest in Him and hear His voice above the noise of life.

And he said, "My presence will go with you,
and I will give you rest."
EXODUS 33:14 ESV

Starting from scratch, he made the entire
human race and made the earth hospitable,
with plenty of time and space for living so
we could seek after God, and not just grope
around in the dark but actually find him.
He doesn't play hide-and-seek with us.
He's not remote; he's near. We live and
move in him, can't get away from him!
ACTS 17:26-28 MSG

The LORD is near to all who call on him,
to all who call on him in truth.
PSALM 145:18 ESV

I believe in the sun even if it isn't shining.
I believe in love even when I am alone.
I believe in God even when He is silent.
UNKNOWN

Before me, even as behind, God is,
and all is well.
JOHN GREENLEAF WHITTIER

Some people talk about
finding God—as if He could get lost.
UNKNOWN

Presence of God

*Blessed are those who have learned to acclaim
you, who walk in the light of your presence, LORD.*
PSALM 89:15 NIV

Close your eyes and imagine yourself sitting on the
beach, a warm breeze tickling your skin and the
comforting sound of waves breaking on the shore. Or
think of yourself in a garden, enchanting fragrances and
the sounds of songbirds in every direction. Place yourself
anywhere, but know that nothing can compare to being
in God's presence. The treasures of the universe are
stored there, His love surrounds you, and peace flows
like a beautiful river. Come and enjoy.

Promises and Fruit

———————

Lord, Your promises are amazing. As I seek You
with all my heart, You show up! Please fill me
to the brim with Your Holy Spirit. Flood me with
love, joy, peace, patience, kindness, goodness,
faithfulness, gentleness, and self-control. I allow
You access to every part of my life, every
part of my home. Teach me and remind me
of who You are and my purpose here on
earth. In Jesus' name, amen.

Show me your ways, Lord, teach me your paths. Guide me in your truth and teach me, for you are God my Savior, and my hope is in you all day long.
Psalm 25:4-5 niv

"But when the Father sends the Advocate as my representative—that is, the Holy Spirit— he will teach you everything and will remind you of everything I have told you."
John 14:26 nlt

"Look! I stand at the door and knock.
If you hear my voice and open the door,
I will come in, and we will share
a meal together as friends."
REVELATION 3:20 NLT

"You will seek me and find me,
when you seek me with all your heart."
JEREMIAH 29:13 ESV

Let us then approach God's throne of grace
with confidence, so that we may receive mercy
and find grace to help us in our time of need.
HEBREWS 4:16 NIV

Character

*[The Lord] guides the humble in what is right
and teaches them his way.*
PSALM 25:9 NIV

The phrase "We're known by the company we keep"
is true regardless of who you hang around with. It's
also true when it's God you're spending time with. As
you rest in His presence, read His words in the Bible,
and talk to Him about all the issues of your life, you
cannot help but take on some of His characteristics. He
is peace, and you become more peaceful. He is good,
and you take on His goodness. You are known by the
company you keep.

The Company
I Keep

Father, I want to be known by the company
I keep because I'm hiding myself in You.
I want to rest in Your presence and live in
Your peace. Allow who You are to rub off on
me. Change me as I come into Your presence
and listen to Your voice. I want to find
You and experience You as much as I
can on this earth. I'm drawing
close to You, God. Amen.

Why do some persons "find" God in a way that others do not? Why does God manifest His presence to some and let multitudes of others struggle along in the half-light of imperfect Christian experience? Of course the will of God is the same for all. He has no favorites within His household. All He has ever done for any of His children He will do for all of His children. The difference lies not with God but with us.

A. W. Tozer

———————

The more we let God take us over, the more truly ourselves we become—because He made us. He invented us. He invented all the different people that you and I were intended to be. . . . It is when I turn to Christ, when I give up myself to His personality, that I first begin to have a real personality of my own.

C. S. Lewis

ETERNAL LIFE

Authentic Faith

But when God, our kind and loving Savior God, stepped in, he saved us from all that. It was all his doing; we had nothing to do with it. He gave us a good bath, and we came out of it new people, washed inside and out by the Holy Spirit. Our Savior Jesus poured out new life so generously. God's gift has restored our relationship with him and given us back our lives. And there's more life to come—an eternity of life! You can count on this.

TITUS 3:7 MSG

What hope do we have for this world if there is no eternity? With no hope, there wouldn't be much to life—we would just live the best we can, and then die. And what if we mess up big before we die? What hope is there if not for Christ?

Faith is believing that Jesus is who He says He is: that God created us, paid for our sins, and is alive today—at work in the hearts and lives of His people. Choosing to live like we believe that needs to look different—not religious, not a nice church supper club full of kind people who do the right thing even when they don't feel like it. Different! Believing that God is at work means living an authentic, Spirit-filled life as the hands and feet of Jesus. And there's more life to come!

For the wages of sin is death, but the free
gift of God is eternal life in
Christ Jesus our Lord.
ROMANS 6:23 ESV

*For the wages of sin is death, but the free
gift of God is eternal life in
Christ Jesus our Lord.*
ROMANS 6:23 ESV

"And this is eternal life, that they know
you, the only true God, and Jesus
Christ whom you have sent."
JOHN 17:3 ESV

"Everyone who calls on the name
of the Lord will be saved."
ROMANS 10:13 ESV

36

Saving faith is an immediate relation to Christ,
accepting, receiving, resting upon Him
alone, for justification, sanctification,
and eternal life by virtue of God's grace.
CHARLES SPURGEON

Since this life is God's and cannot die,
it follows that everyone born anew into
possessing this life is said to have eternal life.
WATCHMAN NEE

Among the many signs of a lively faith and
hope we have in eternal life, one of the surest
is not being overly sad at the death of
those whom we dearly love in our Lord.
IGNATIUS

Eternal Life

God so loved the world that he gave his one and only Son, that whoever believes in him shall not perish but have eternal life.
JOHN 3:16 NIV

Life here on earth is fleeting. One day we are sitting on the floor playing with our favorite dolls, and then we find ourselves grown-up women dealing with grown-up issues. In what seems like a moment, we notice gray hair and wrinkles tickling the borders of our once youthful faces. Fortunately, we have the promise of eternal life. God created a way for us to live on, free from time and age. Through the death of His Son, He purchased eternal life for you. What greater gift could there be? Have you accepted it?

Leaning In

God, You have promised me an inheritance
that can never perish, spoil, or fade, kept in
heaven for me (1 Peter 1:4-5). You tell me that
I am shielded by Your power as I await Your
return. I rejoice in this, even though life is
hard here. Show me Your ways as I lean into
You. I trust Your promises for me. Let me
live like I believe that! Amen.

"Truly, truly, I say to you, whoever hears my
word and believes him who sent me has
eternal life. He does not come into judgment,
but has passed from death to life."
JOHN 5:24 ESV

I eagerly expect and hope that I will in
no way be ashamed, but will have sufficient
courage so that now as always Christ
will be exalted in my body,
whether by life or by death.
PHILIPPIANS 1:20 NIV

"There is salvation in no one else,
for there is no other name under heaven
given among men by which we must be saved."
ACTS 4:12 ESV

For by grace you have been saved
through faith. And this is not your own
doing; it is the gift of God, not a result
of works, so that no one may boast.
EPHESIANS 2:8-9 ESV

"I'm telling you the most solemn and sober
truth now: Whoever believes in me has real
life, eternal life. I am the Bread of Life."
JOHN 6:50-51 MSG

The Lord is not slow to fulfill his promise as
some count slowness, but is patient toward
you, not wishing that any should perish,
but that all should reach repentance.
2 PETER 3:9 ESV

Sealed by His Promise

*"My sheep listen to my voice; I know them,
and they follow me. I give them eternal life,
and they will never die, and no one
can steal them out of my hand."*
JOHN 10:27-28 NCV

In eternity we will have no need of protection. All will be well as we occupy the heavenly kingdom. But here on earth we are subject to many hazards. God has not left your eternal life to chance. He purchased it for you with the sacrifice of His own Son. He Himself watches over you so that nothing and no one can keep you from reaching your destination. The life God has given you is not up for the taking. It is sealed by His promise.

Amazing Love

What amazing love you have blessed us with,
Father! A love I do not deserve. Let my heart
be filled with love for You so that I can share
this great blessing with others. You are my
hope in an often hopeless world. You are
my hope of heaven, my hope of peace,
my hope of change, purpose,
and unconditional love. Amen.

*Beware of the pleasant view of the fatherhood
of God: God is so kind and loving that of
course He will forgive us. That thought,
based solely on emotion, cannot be found
anywhere in the New Testament. The only
basis on which God can forgive us is the
tremendous tragedy of the Cross of Christ.*

OSWALD CHAMBERS

---

*The purpose of His life, death, and resurrection
was to ransom you from your sin, deliver you
from the clutches of evil, restore you to God—
so that His personality and His life could heal
and fill your personality, your humanity,
and your life. This is the reason
He came. Anything else is religion.*

JOHN ELDREDGE

WHO I AM
IN CHRIST

For our sake he made him to be sin who knew no sin, so that in him we might become the righteousness of God.

2 Corinthians 5:21 ESV

Many Christians go most of their lives without knowing and believing who they truly are in Christ. They go to church, join a small group, lead a Bible study, do a lot of great things—but they miss the abundant life that is available to them. There is more to life than church groups and religious endeavors. So much more!

God's Word teaches us that the same power that raised Jesus from the grave lives in us as believers (Romans 8:11; Ephesians 1:19-20)! When God looks at us, He sees the righteousness of Christ. He is not a giant emoji in the sky—happy when we do right, disappointed when we get it wrong, mad when we get it really wrong. No! He sees us as righteous every single moment. Don't take the cross of Christ for granted. Don't make less of it, ever! Hebrews 10:10 tells us that God's will was for us to be made holy by the sacrifice of the body of Jesus Christ, once for all time. The death of Christ made us 100 percent right with God—once and for all.

Now it's time to live your life *believing* who you are in Christ! What does that mean for you? How will that change the way you think, feel, and interact with others? Take those questions to God. He is waiting to show you the answer!

See what kind of love the Father has given to us, that we should be called children of God; and so we are. The reason why the world does not know us is that it did not know him.
1 JOHN 3:1 ESV

For we are God's masterpiece. He has created us anew in Christ Jesus, so we can do the good things he planned for us long ago.
EPHESIANS 2:10 NLT

And I am sure of this, that he who began a good work in you will bring it to completion at the day of Jesus Christ.
PHILIPPIANS 1:6 ESV

My hope is built on nothing less
Than Jesus' blood and righteousness.
I dare not trust the sweetest frame,
But wholly lean on Jesus' name.
When darkness seems to hide His face,
I rest on His unchanging grace.
In every high and stormy gale,
My anchor holds within the veil.
When He shall come with trumpet sound,
O may I then in Him be found!
Dressed in His righteousness alone,
Faultless to stand before the throne!

EDWARD MOTE

Righteousness

*The work of righteousness shall be
peace; and the effect of righteousness
quietness and assurance for ever.*
ISAIAH 32:17 KJV

What a comfort it is to know that God has paid the price for all your mistakes and declared you righteous based on the life of His own flawless Son. When the enemy comes to condemn you, the blood of Jesus stands between you and anything the devil accuses you of. Jesus paid the price and God found you righteous—without blame. Rest assured that God is on your side. You have been cleared of any wrongdoing by the highest court. You are right in God's eyes.

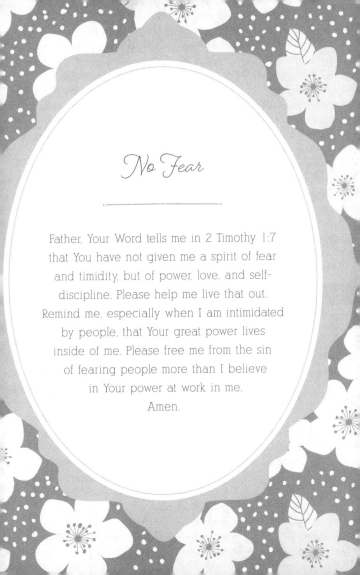

No Fear

Father, Your Word tells me in 2 Timothy 1:7
that You have not given me a spirit of fear
and timidity, but of power, love, and self-
discipline. Please help me live that out.
Remind me, especially when I am intimidated
by people, that Your great power lives
inside of me. Please free me from the sin
of fearing people more than I believe
in Your power at work in me.
Amen.

But to all who believed him and accepted him,
he gave the right to become children of God.
<small>JOHN 1:12 NLT</small>

Don't you realize that your body is the temple
of the Holy Spirit, who lives in you and was
given to you by God? You do not belong
to yourself, for God bought you with a high
price. So you must honor God with your body.
<small>1 CORINTHIANS 6:19–20 NLT</small>

But you belong to God, my dear children.
You have already won a victory over those
people, because the Spirit who lives in you is
greater than the spirit who lives in the world.
<small>1 JOHN 4:4 NLT</small>

*This resurrection life you received from
God is not a timid, grave-tending life.
It's adventurously expectant, greeting
God with a childlike "What's next, Papa?"
God's Spirit touches our spirits and confirms
who we really are. We know who he is,
and we know who we are: Father and
children. And we know we are going
to get what's coming to us—an
unbelievable inheritance!*
ROMANS 8:15-16 MSG

*"I am the vine; you are the branches.
Whoever abides in me and I in him,
he it is that bears much fruit, for apart
from me you can do nothing."*
JOHN 15:5 ESV

The Right Path

*The way of the righteous is like the first gleam
of dawn, which shines ever brighter
until the full light of day.*
PROVERBS 4:18 NLT

God knows where you're going. As you journey on
the road toward God's purpose and plan for your life,
the light of God's love grows brighter with each step,
bringing you closer and closer to Him. The more you
know Him, the more quickly you know His will and His
ways and can more assuredly step out in faith toward
His righteous cause. Your steps are sure because your
path is well lit with the goodness of God. You're on
the right path.

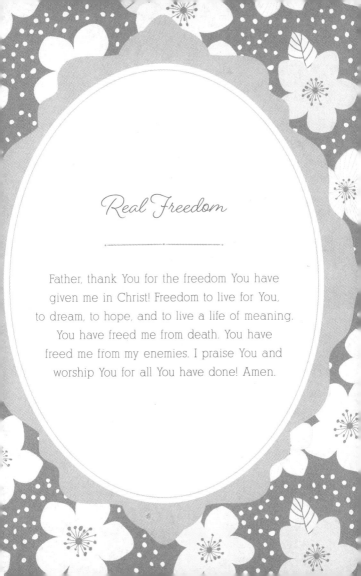

Real Freedom

Father, thank You for the freedom You have
given me in Christ! Freedom to live for You,
to dream, to hope, and to live a life of meaning.
You have freed me from death. You have
freed me from my enemies. I praise You and
worship You for all You have done! Amen.

*May we think of freedom, not as the
right to do as we please, but as the
opportunity to do what is right.*
PETER MARSHALL

*Divine love is perfect peace and joy,
it is a freedom from all disquiet, it is all
content and happiness; and makes
everything to rejoice in itself.*
WILLIAM LAW

FREEDOM

True Peace

It is for freedom that Christ has set us free.
Stand firm, then, and do not let yourselves
be burdened again by a yoke of slavery.

GALATIANS 5:1 NIV

Freedom in Christ is more than just being free from sin and securing our place in heaven. Freedom in Christ means that we can be free here and now—to live a life of purpose, to hope and to dream. We don't have to be imprisoned by negative thinking or worried about what others think of us. We don't have to watch our backs or concern ourselves over idle gossip. Freedom in Christ gives us confidence to be all that God made us to be.

If someone is trying to stifle your freedom in Christ, run to God about it. Ask Him to show you His truth. No one has the right to tell you who you are except your Creator. Search His Word and ask the Holy Spirit to be your guide as you search for freedom. God confirms His truth. If you believe God is telling you something, ask Him to confirm it, and then relax while He does. He wants to tell you the truth about who He is and who you are in Him!

As believers, we are no longer held captive by fear. The perfect love that Christ offers us casts out all fear (1 John 4:18), and we can have true peace—a peace that transcends all understanding—here on earth while we live our daily lives. When we live like we are free in Christ, our insecurities fade, our fears diminish, and love takes over.

Now the Lord is the Spirit, and where the Spirit of the Lord is, there is freedom.

2 Corinthians 3:17 esv

There is therefore now no condemnation for those who are in Christ Jesus. For the law of the Spirit of life has set you free in Christ Jesus from the law of sin and death.

Romans 8:1-2 esv

Live as people who are free, not using your freedom as a cover-up for evil, but living as servants of God.

1 Peter 2:16 esv

To serve God, to love God, to enjoy God,
is the sweetest freedom in the world.
Thomas Watson

In almost everything that touches our
everyday life on earth, God is pleased
when we're pleased. He wills that we be
as free as birds to soar and sing our
maker's praise without anxiety.
A. W. Tozer

Freedom

The LORD sets prisoners free.
PSALM 146:7 NIV

Some women run from God, thinking He will ask them to surrender their freedom and lock them down to some religious regimen. In reality, just the opposite is true. We are all already in bondage to our unwashed thoughts and behaviors and our sinful nature. Before you can flourish in God's kingdom, He has to remove your bonds. Fortunately, your heavenly Father is in the chain-breaking business. Ask Him to set you free.

Free from Bondage

God, Your Word tells me that the creation itself
will be set free from its bondage to corruption
and will obtain the freedom of the glory of
the children of God (Romans 8:21). I do not
want to live in bondage any longer. Bondage
can camouflage itself, so please give me
discernment to recognize bondage when I
feel it. You offer freedom from everything
that holds me back from an abundant
life with You. Help me live in that
freedom each day. Amen.

*For you were called to freedom, brothers.
Only do not use your freedom as an
opportunity for the flesh, but through
love serve one another.*
GALATIANS 5:13 ESV

---

*The Spirit of the Lord GOD is upon me,
because the LORD has anointed me to bring
good news to the poor; he has sent me to
bind up the brokenhearted, to proclaim
liberty to the captives, and the opening
of the prison to those who are bound.*
ISAIAH 61:1 ESV

*But now you are free from the power
of sin and have become slaves of God.
Now you do those things that lead to
holiness and result in eternal life.*
ROMANS 6:22 NLT

*But now that you've found you don't have
to listen to sin tell you what to do, and have
discovered the delight of listening to God
telling you, what a surprise! A whole, healed,
put-together life right now, with more and
more of life on the way! Work hard for sin
your whole life and your pension is death.
But God's gift is real life, eternal life,
delivered by Jesus, our Master.*
ROMANS 6:22-23 MSG

Freedom Follows

The Lord is the Spirit, and where the Spirit
of the Lord is, there is freedom.
2 CORINTHIANS 3:17 ESV

Wherever the Spirit of God goes, freedom follows. If His Spirit dwells in you, you will experience more freedom than you have ever known. You will no longer be inhibited by selfishness and resentment. You will be free to do what you were created to do—live in right relationship with your Creator. Don't struggle to free yourself. You haven't the power or the strength. Invite God's Holy Spirit to come inside your heart and free you in the process.

Set Me Free

Set me free, Lord, set me free! Sometimes
I live captive by my own thoughts and fears.
But I trust that You can help me overcome
my insecurities and live with my heart set
on You. Father, help me to get over self-doubt.
Remind me that Your blessings are forever
and I have nothing to fear. Amen.

To be risen with Christ means not only that
one has a choice and that one may live by
a higher law—the law of grace and love—but
that one must do so. The first obligation of
the Christian is to maintain their freedom
from all superstitions, all blind taboos
and religious formalities, indeed
from all empty forms of legalism.

THOMAS MERTON

ARMOR
OF GOD

Daily Battle

———————

Put on the full armor of God, so that you can take your stand against the devil's schemes. For our struggle is not against flesh and blood, but against the rulers, against the authorities, against the powers of this dark world and against the spiritual forces of evil in the heavenly realms. Therefore put on the full armor of God, so that when the day of evil comes, you may be able to stand your ground, and after you have done everything, to stand.

EPHESIANS 6:11–13 NIV

Get in the habit of putting on your armor daily. Visualize yourself buckling the belt of truth around your waist so you won't believe any lies of the enemy. Put on the breastplate of righteousness, reminding yourself that you are covered in the righteousness of Christ. Put on the shoes of the gospel of peace, ready to share your faith with anyone God puts in your path. Take up your shield of faith in a powerful God who extinguishes the fiery darts of the enemy. Put on your helmet of salvation with your mind set on things above, ready to take captive every thought to Christ. And finally wield the sword of the Spirit, which is God's Word. As you hide His Word in your heart, the Holy Spirit will remind you of each truth as you need it throughout your daily battle. Fight back with the Word of God and speak it out loud as you need to. You are now thoroughly prepared to face anything that comes your way.

*My dear children, you come from God
and belong to God. You have already won
a big victory over those false teachers,
for the Spirit in you is far stronger
than anything in the world.*
1 JOHN 4:4 MSG

*So humble yourselves before God.
Resist the devil, and he will flee from you.*
JAMES 4:7 NLT

*I am worn out waiting for your rescue,
but I have put my hope in your word.*
PSALM 119:81 NLT

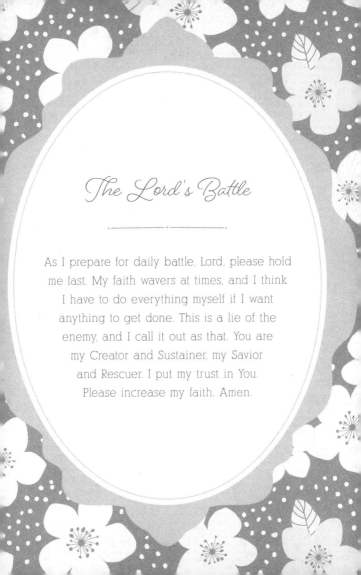

The Lord's Battle

As I prepare for daily battle, Lord, please hold
me fast. My faith wavers at times, and I think
I have to do everything myself if I want
anything to get done. This is a lie of the
enemy, and I call it out as that. You are
my Creator and Sustainer, my Savior
and Rescuer. I put my trust in You.
Please increase my faith. Amen.

Stand firm then, with the belt of truth buckled around your waist, with the breastplate of righteousness in place, and with your feet fitted with the readiness that comes from the gospel of peace. In addition to all this, take up the shield of faith, with which you can extinguish all the flaming arrows of the evil one. Take the helmet of salvation and the sword of the Spirit, which is the word of God.
EPHESIANS 6:14-17 NIV

*Remember your promise to me;
it is my only hope.*
PSALM 119:49 NLT

Pray often, for prayer is a shield to the soul,
a sacrifice to God, and a scourge for Satan.
JOHN BUNYAN

Our prayers should be for blessings in general,
for God knows best what is good for us.
SOCRATES

God knows what He is doing, and there is
nothing accidental in the life of the
believer. Nothing but good can come
to those who are wholly His.
WATCHMAN NEE

On to Victory!

Our struggle is not against flesh and blood,
but against the rulers, against the authorities,
against the powers of this dark world and
against the spiritual forces of evil
in the heavenly realms.
EPHESIANS 6:12 NIV

In God's kingdom, women are called to be warriors. Alongside their Christian brothers, they are asked to battle with the forces of evil that plot to destroy human lives and keep them from knowing their Creator. This is warfare fought in the spiritual realm with an enemy we know is there but whom we cannot see. Put on your spiritual armor and ask God to point out your battle station. And then—on to victory!

My Life Is in Your Hands

Father God, how amazing it is to me that You are the Creator of the universe, the one who placed the stars in the sky, yet You care for me deeply! When I put my life in Your hands, I am safe. When I'm covered in Your armor, I'm prepared. Thank You for Your great love and provision for me. Amen.

*For though we live in the world, we do not
wage war as the world does. The weapons we
fight with are not the weapons of the world.
On the contrary, they have divine power to
demolish strongholds. We demolish arguments
and every pretension that sets itself
up against the knowledge of God,
and we take captive every thought
to make it obedient to Christ.*
2 Corinthians 10:3-5 niv

---

*God can't break his word. And because his
word cannot change, the promise is likewise
unchangeable. We who have run for our
very lives to God have every reason
to grab the promised hope with
both hands and never let go.*
Hebrews 6:18 msg

To be in God's keeping is surely a blessing,
For though life is often dark and depressing,
No day is too dark and no burden too great
That God in His love cannot penetrate.

HELEN STEINER RICE

Spiritual Protection

*Put on the full armor of God, so that you can
take your stand against the devil's schemes.*
EPHESIANS 6:11 NIV

It's a good idea for every woman to take a basic
class in self-defense in order to protect herself in this
predator-filled world. A wise woman will learn how to
defend herself spiritually, as well. God has provided
you with a full suit of armor for that purpose—truth,
righteousness, peace, faith, and salvation. Wear them
everywhere you go. You do have an enemy, and he
wants to take all you have. Be prepared to resist and
defeat him.

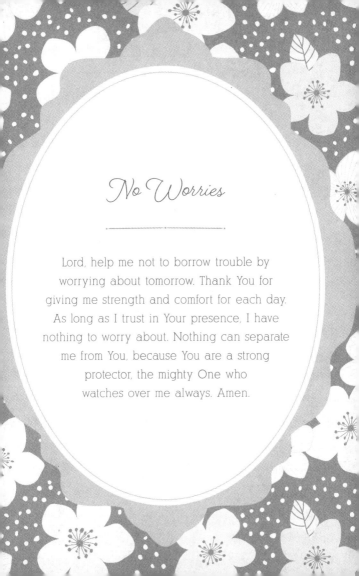

No Worries

Lord, help me not to borrow trouble by
worrying about tomorrow. Thank You for
giving me strength and comfort for each day.
As long as I trust in Your presence, I have
nothing to worry about. Nothing can separate
me from You, because You are a strong
protector, the mighty One who
watches over me always. Amen.

*The devil is a better theologian
than any of us and is a devil still.*
A. W. TOZER

—————— · ——————

*Beware of no man more than of yourself,
for we often carry our worst
enemies within us.*
CHARLES SPURGEON

—————— · ——————

*If we had no winter, the spring would not be
so pleasant: If we did not sometimes taste of
adversity, prosperity would not be so welcome.*
ANNE BRADSTREET

DAILY WALK

Possible with God

Rejoice always, pray without ceasing, give thanks in all circumstances; for this is the will of God in Christ Jesus for you.
1 THESSALONIANS 5:16-18 ESV

Ever wonder what God's will is for you? First Thessalonians spells it out for us right here: rejoice always, pray continually, and give thanks in all circumstances. How can we possibly do this? The only way we can carry out God's will in our daily walk is through the power of Christ working in us. It is not humanly possible to be joyful always—but God's Spirit can help us to find joy in the presence of Christ even during the darkest of times. Even during suffering—because we know He is with us. It is not humanly possible to pray without ceasing; how would we ever sleep? But we can be in constant communion with God, having an attitude of prayer and a deep trust in God as we fall asleep. It may not be humanly possible to give thanks *for* your current circumstances—but you can thank Him *in* the circumstance, knowing that He is greater than the evil you may be facing and that He will work out everything for your good.

All of these things are possible with God's power at work within us. For what is impossible with man is possible with God (Luke 18:27)!

I remain confident of this: I will see the goodness of the LORD in the land of the living. Wait for the LORD; be strong and take heart and wait for the LORD.
PSALM 27:13-14 NIV

The LORD gives strength to his people; the LORD blesses his people with peace.
PSALM 29:11 NIV

Jesus Christ is the same yesterday and today and forever.
HEBREWS 13:8 NIV

Shout for joy, you heavens; rejoice, you earth; burst into song, you mountains! For the LORD comforts his people and will have compassion on his afflicted ones.
ISAIAH 49:13 NIV

I Am Loved

Father, when troubles come, I never have
to face them alone. You are my refuge and
strength. You comfort me in times of trouble,
and You watch over me from day to day. I tell
You my problems and You listen, Lord. I speak
of the good things in my life and You smile.
I ask You for advice, knowing it will come
in Your time. I am no longer lonely;
I am loved. Amen.

For the word of the LORD is right and true;
he is faithful in all he does.
PSALM 33:4 NIV

We put our hope in the LORD. He is our
help and our shield. In him our hearts
rejoice, for we trust in his holy name.
Let your unfailing love surround us,
LORD, for our hope is in you alone.
PSALM 33:20-22 NLT

"No wonder my heart is glad, and my tongue
shouts his praises! My body rests in hope."
ACTS 2:26 NLT

God didn't promise days without pain,
laughter without sorrow, sun without rain,
but He did promise strength for the day,
comfort for the tears, and light for the way.
ANONYMOUS

God never built a Christian strong enough
to carry today's duties and tomorrow's
anxieties piled on top of them.
THEODORE LEDYARD CUYLER

What a friend we have in Jesus,
All our sins and griefs to bear.
What a privilege to carry
Everything to God in prayer.
JOSEPH SCRIVEN

Daily Walk

Just as you received Christ Jesus as Lord, continue
to live your lives in him, rooted and built up in him,
strengthened in the faith as you were taught,
and overflowing with thankfulness.
COLOSSIANS 2:6-7 NIV

Even though you don't always see progress in your walk with God, you can be sure that your roots are going down deep. Beneath the soil, God tends your faith—the longer you walk with Him, the deeper His hold on you. You came to Him with nothing and simply surrendered to His love. And that is all it takes—just a willingness to keep walking with Him and trusting that He is strengthening your roots beneath you.

The Center of My Day

When I set my mind on You, heavenly Father,
I am much more aware of the simple and many
ways You bless me every day. Be the center of
my day so that I don't miss out on what You
want to show me. I don't want to dwell on what
might happen in the future; I want to relish
this chance to nurture and cherish the
blessings You have given me. Amen.

Love the LORD your God with all your heart and with all your soul and with all your strength. These commandments that I give you today are to be on your hearts. Impress them on your children. Talk about them when you sit at home and when you walk along the road, when you lie down and when you get up. Tie them as symbols on your hands and bind them on your foreheads. Write them on the doorframes of your houses and on your gates.

DEUTERONOMY 6:5-9 NIV

Since, then, you have been raised with Christ, set your hearts on things above, where Christ is, seated at the right hand of God. Set your minds on things above, not on earthly things.

COLOSSIANS 3:1-2 NIV

For the invasion of my soul by Thy Holy Spirit:
for all human love and goodness that
speaks to me of Thee: for the fullness
of Thy glory outpoured in Jesus Christ,
I give Thee thanks, O God.

JOHN BAILLIE

Life stands before me like an eternal
spring with new and brilliant clothes.

CARL FRIEDRICH GAUSS

Faith is a virtue by which, clinging to the
faithfulness of God, we lean upon Him so
that we may obtain what He gives us.

WILLIAM AMES

93

Crossroads

Be very careful, then,
how you live—not as unwise but as wise.
EPHESIANS 5:15 NIV

As you walk with the Lord each day, you will face many crossroads. God will open the way before you, but He will not mandate your steps. He has given you a free will with which to choose the steps you take. He does admonish you to choose wisely, though. The safest way to do that is to keep your hand in God's hand at all times. He will never let you wander off the path. Reach out to Him, and He will be there.

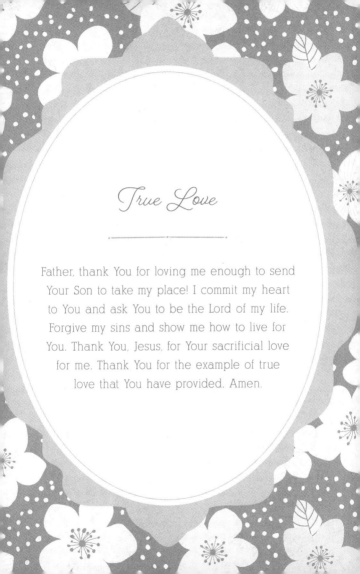

True Love

Father, thank You for loving me enough to send
Your Son to take my place! I commit my heart
to You and ask You to be the Lord of my life.
Forgive my sins and show me how to live for
You. Thank You, Jesus, for Your sacrificial love
for me. Thank You for the example of true
love that You have provided. Amen.

Standing on the promises of Christ the Lord,
Bound to Him eternally by love's strong cord,
Overcoming daily with the Spirit's sword,
Standing on the promises of God.

R. KELSO CARTER

———————

The sun. . .in its full glory, either at rising or
setting—this and many other like blessings
we enjoy daily; and for the most of them,
because they are so common, most men
forget to pay their praises. But let us not.

IZAAK WALTON

FAMILY

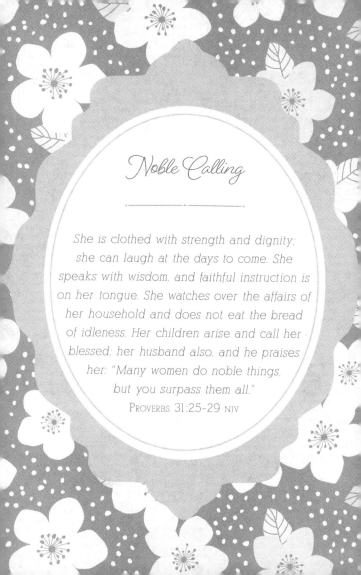

Noble Calling

*She is clothed with strength and dignity;
she can laugh at the days to come. She
speaks with wisdom, and faithful instruction is
on her tongue. She watches over the affairs of
her household and does not eat the bread
of idleness. Her children arise and call her
blessed; her husband also, and he praises
her: "Many women do noble things,
but you surpass them all."*
PROVERBS 31:25-29 NIV

Wouldn't it be fabulous if your children would arise and call you *blessed* every morning? Most days a mom has to stir cranky kids out of bed (sometimes with great effort and force!), try to get them to eat something that resembles a healthy breakfast, and rush them through the brushing of their teeth and changing into (hopefully) clean clothes before the bus comes. The kids usually forget the "calling mom blessed" part.

Being a mom is a noble (and difficult and stressful and exciting and emotional and exhausting and priceless and wonderful) calling. Hannah Whitall Smith said, "The mother is and must be—whether she knows it or not—the greatest, strongest, and most lasting teacher her children have." Whew! That's a lot of pressure! But that's just the thing: we cannot do it alone—and we're not expected to! We need the power of Christ to strengthen us to do this colossal job, and He is with us during every moment.

Remember moms: you are never alone! God is with you and available to you at all times and during every situation you find yourself in with your children. Your children are ultimately in God's hands. Worry less. Pray more!

*Love is patient and kind; love does not envy
or boast; it is not arrogant or rude. It does
not insist on its own way; it is not irritable
or resentful; it does not rejoice at wrongdoing,
but rejoices with the truth. Love bears
all things, believes all things, hopes
all things, endures all things.*
1 Corinthians 13:4-7 esv

*Bearing with one another and, if one
has a complaint against another, forgiving
each other; as the Lord has forgiven
you, so you also must forgive.*
Colossians 3:13 esv

A Thankful Heart

Create a thankful heart in me, Father. I need
Your gentle wisdom for every area of my life.
I'm so thankful that what You offer is the best.
Thank You for my family. Thank You for friends
who have become my family. Thank You for
always providing for me. Thank You! Amen.

We love because he first loved us.
1 JOHN 4:19 ESV

However, let each one of you love his wife
as himself, and let the wife see that
she respects her husband.
EPHESIANS 5:33 ESV

Children are a gift from the LORD; they are
a reward from him. Children born to a
young man are like arrows in a
warrior's hands. How joyful is the
man whose quiver is full of them!
PSALM 127:3-5 NLT

Train up a child in the way he should go;
even when he is old he will not depart from it.
PROVERBS 22:6 ESV

Train up a child in the way he should go—
but be sure you go that way yourself.
CHARLES SPURGEON

Nothing can bring a real sense of security
into the home except true love.
BILLY GRAHAM

A man ought to live so that everybody knows
he is a Christian. . .and most of all,
his family ought to know.
D. L. MOODY

103

The Influence of a Woman

A wise woman strengthens her family.
PROVERBS 14:1 NCV

The influence of a woman on her family is phenomenal—for good and for bad. Sadly, some women weaken their families through selfishness, ambition, and carelessness. The vigilant, wise, and godly woman holds her family together, makes sacrifices to ensure its stability, and entreats God's blessing with her prayers. You can be that kind of woman—the kind that builds up and strengthens. Ask God to help you. He will show you how.

Abundantly Blessed

Heavenly Father, thank You for the simple
joys of life: my health, my family, my friends.
Help me to slow down and appreciate all the
blessings in my life. You have provided me
with everything I need and have blessed me
abundantly. Help me delight in the little
gifts You bring my way every day. Amen.

But if anyone does not provide for his
relatives, and especially for members of
his household, he has denied the faith
and is worse than an unbeliever.
1 TIMOTHY 5:8 ESV

"And I will be a father to you, and you
shall be sons and daughters to me,
says the Lord Almighty."
2 CORINTHIANS 6:18 ESV

God places the lonely in families;
he sets the prisoners free and gives them
joy. But he makes the rebellious
live in a sun-scorched land.
PSALM 68:6 NLT

*If therefore our houses be houses of the Lord,
we shall for that reason love home, reckoning
our daily devotion the sweetest of our daily
delights; and our family-worship the most
valuable of our family-comforts. . . . A church
in the house will be a good legacy,
nay, it will be a good inheritance,
to be left to your children after you.*

MATTHEW HENRY

---

*It may not be an easy thing to live in
sweet fellowship with all those with whom
we come in contact; but that is what
the grace of God is given to us for.*

D. L. MOODY

In this way we are like the various parts of a human body. Each part gets its meaning from the body as a whole, not the other way around. The body we're talking about is Christ's body of chosen people. Each of us finds our meaning and function as a part of his body. But as a chopped-off finger or cut-off toe we wouldn't amount to much, would we? So since we find ourselves fashioned into all these excellently formed and marvelously functioning parts in Christ's body, let's just go ahead and be what we were made to be, without enviously or pridefully comparing ourselves with each other, or trying to be something we aren't.

Romans 12:4-6 MSG

FRIENDSHIP

Blessing of Friendship

Finally, all of you should be of one mind.
Sympathize with each other. Love each other as
brothers and sisters. Be tenderhearted, and keep
a humble attitude. Don't repay evil for evil.
Don't retaliate with insults when people insult
you. Instead, pay them back with a blessing.
That is what God has called you to do,
and he will grant you his blessing.

1 PETER 3:8-9 NLT

Thank God for the blessing of friendship! Jesus gives us the ultimate example of what friendship really is: laying down His life for ours so that we might lay down our lives for another. That's love. That's true friendship. Ask God for help to be that kind of friend.

God wants us to be tender and humble in our friendships—never retaliating when we are hurt but offering a blessing instead. Do you want God's blessing on your life? Pay back people with blessings even when they don't deserve it. Our faith increases as we encourage our friends and serve God together in this way.

And guess what? God's Word tells us in John 15 that He calls *us* friend! What an honor that He would choose us and love us unconditionally. Now you can say to yourself, *I am a friend of God!* Ask God to let His love shine through you so that you bear fruit that will last in your friendships.

*Two are better than one, because they have
a good reward for their toil. For if they fall,
one will lift up his fellow. But woe to him who
is alone when he falls and has not another to
lift him up! Again, if two lie together, they
keep warm, but how can one keep warm
alone? And though a man might prevail
against one who is alone, two will
withstand him—a threefold
cord is not quickly broken.*

ECCLESIASTES 4:9-12 ESV

For health and food, for love and friends,
For everything Thy goodness sends,
Father in heaven, we thank Thee.
RALPH WALDO EMERSON

I thank God for all things good—peace,
happiness, laughter, and friends.
BONNIE JENSEN

It is one of the blessings of old friends
that you can afford to be stupid with them.
RALPH WALDO EMERSON

Friendship

A friend loves at all times. They are there
to help when trouble comes.
PROVERBS 17:17 NIRV

Tough times reveal real friends. Partly that is true because real friends are the ones who stick around when things are troublesome and uncomfortable and not at all fun. But also it is true because, when you are at your worst or weakest, you can only bear to be witnessed by real friends—those who already know you inside and out and accept you just the way you are. Ask God to give you that kind of friend.

Freedom in Friendship

Father God, thank You that in Your great
wisdom, You didn't want me to be alone.
You are always with me, and You have blessed
me with the gift of friendship. Please bring
good friends into my life, friends that bring
freedom and refreshment. Help me honor
You in my friendships. Amen.

"Greater love has no one than this, that
someone lay down his life for his friends."
JOHN 15:13 ESV

Therefore encourage one another and build
one another up, just as you are doing.
1 THESSALONIANS 5:11 ESV

Oil and perfume make the heart glad,
and the sweetness of a friend comes
from his earnest counsel.
PROVERBS 27:9 ESV

Do not be deceived:
"Bad company ruins good morals."
1 Corinthians 15:33 esv

* * *

Love prospers when a fault is forgiven,
but dwelling on it separates close friends.
Proverbs 17:9 nlt

* * *

A troublemaker plants seeds of strife;
gossip separates the best of friends.
Proverbs 16:28 nlt

Truth

Speaking the truth in love. . .grow up into him
in all things, which is the head, even Christ.
EPHESIANS 4:15 KJV

Heated words really stress relationships. A white lie may seem more easily swallowed than the blunt truth of a situation, but God has blessed you with the help of His Holy Spirit to bring truth into the lives of others. He knows their hearts and the words that should be spoken to bring them closer to God and to you. Truth mixed with love is a rich treasure, and when it overflows out of your heart, it becomes a beautiful gift to those around you.

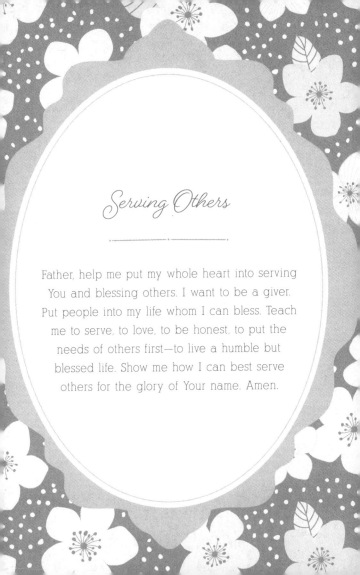

Serving Others

Father, help me put my whole heart into serving You and blessing others. I want to be a giver. Put people into my life whom I can bless. Teach me to serve, to love, to be honest, to put the needs of others first—to live a humble but blessed life. Show me how I can best serve others for the glory of Your name. Amen.

Don't hang out with angry people;
don't keep company with hotheads.
Bad temper is contagious—don't get infected.
PROVERBS 22:24-25 MSG

Wounds from a sincere friend are better
than many kisses from an enemy.
PROVERBS 27:6 NLT

When we get together, I want to encourage
you in your faith, but I also want to
be encouraged by yours.
ROMANS 1:12 NLT

Friendship is always a sweet responsibility,
never an opportunity.
KHALIL GIBRAN

God, who is love. . .simply cannot help
but shed blessing upon blessing upon us.
We do not need to beg, for He
simply cannot help it!
HANNAH WHITALL SMITH

Love is the only force capable of
transforming an enemy into a friend.
MARTIN LUTHER KING JR.

And let us consider how we may spur one another on toward love and good deeds, not giving up meeting together, as some are in the habit of doing, but encouraging one another—and all the more as you see the Day approaching.
HEBREWS 10:24-25 NIV

Above all, keep loving one another earnestly, since love covers a multitude of sins. Show hospitality to one another without grumbling. As each has received a gift, use it to serve one another, as good stewards of God's varied grace.
1 PETER 4:8-10 ESV

PRAISE BRINGS
PEACE

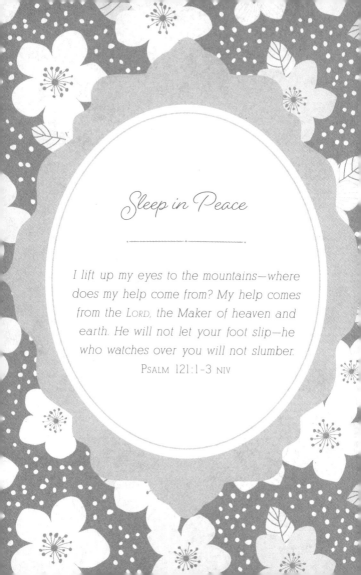

Sleep in Peace

I lift up my eyes to the mountains—where does my help come from? My help comes from the LORD, the Maker of heaven and earth. He will not let your foot slip—he who watches over you will not slumber.

PSALM 121:1-3 NIV

Where has God been through all of this? You may ask. *It's been hard. Too hard. How could He let any of this happen?*

Evangelical Christian author Philip Yancey, in *Where Is God When It Hurts?*, says that God has been there from the very beginning. He joins us in our suffering; He hurts with us—sharing in our pain. And in the midst of our suffering, His Spirit offers peace and comfort. In Luke 12:32, after telling us how useless it is to worry, Jesus says, "Do not be afraid, little flock, for your Father has been pleased to give you the kingdom" (NIV). Can't you hear and feel the love in God's heart for you? When life hurts, give it to Jesus. In Matthew 11:28 He says, "Come to me, all of you who are weary and carry heavy burdens, and I will give you rest" (NLT). *Rest!* How we need rest.

So, as Victor Hugo aptly said, "Have courage for the great sorrows in life, and patience for the small ones. And when you have laboriously accomplished your daily tasks, go to sleep in peace, God is awake."

Let all that I am praise the LORD; with my whole
heart, I will praise his holy name. Let all that
I am praise the LORD; may I never forget
the good things he does for me.
PSALM 103:1-2 NLT

I have seen you in your sanctuary and gazed
upon your power and glory. Your unfailing
love is better than life itself; how I praise you!
I will praise you as long as I live, lifting up
my hands to you in prayer. You satisfy me
more than the richest feast. I will
praise you with songs of joy.
PSALM 63:2-5 NLT

Worship the LORD with gladness.
Come before him, singing with joy.
PSALM 100:2 NLT

Turn your eyes upon Jesus,
Look full in His wonderful face,
And the things of earth will grow strangely dim
In the light of His glory and grace.
HELEN HOWARTH LEMMEL

If God hath made this world so fair,
Where sin and death abound,
How beautiful beyond compare
Will paradise be found!
JAMES MONTGOMERY

127

Free Expression

I will praise You, O Lord, with my whole heart. . . .
I will sing praise to Your name, O Most High.
PSALM 9:1-2 NKJV

Your life is a form of praise, but your words of praise
are even more precious to your heavenly Father. His
Holy Spirit who lives within you carries them straight
to His throne. Why are your praises so dear to Him?
Because they are the free expression of your heart.
You chose Him when you could have chosen so many
others. Lift your voice to Him. It brings Him great joy.

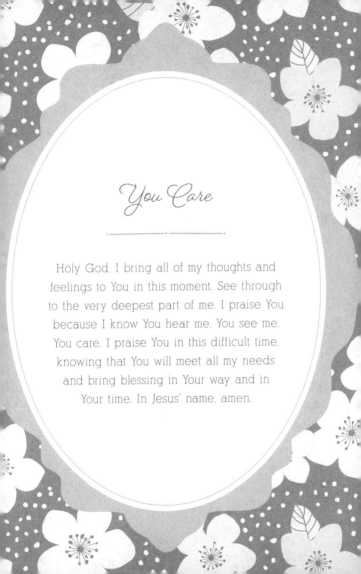

You Care

Holy God, I bring all of my thoughts and feelings to You in this moment. See through to the very deepest part of me. I praise You because I know You hear me. You see me. You care. I praise You in this difficult time, knowing that You will meet all my needs and bring blessing in Your way and in Your time. In Jesus' name, amen.

How great is the goodness you have stored up for those who fear you. You lavish it on those who come to you for protection, blessing them before the watching world. You hide them in the shelter of your presence, safe from those who conspire against them. You shelter them in your presence, far from accusing tongues. Praise the LORD, for he has shown me the wonders of his unfailing love.

PSALM 31:19-21 NLT

Don't worry about anything; instead, pray about everything. Tell God what you need, and thank him for all he has done. Then you will experience God's peace, which exceeds anything we can understand. His peace will guard your hearts and minds as you live in Christ Jesus.

PHILIPPIANS 4:6-7 NLT

*Prayer is. . .a mine which is never
exhausted. . . . It is the root, the fountain,
the mother of a thousand blessings.*
JOHN CHRYSOSTOM

---

*We would worry less if we praised
more. Thanksgiving is the enemy of
discontent and dissatisfaction.*
HARRY IRONSIDE

---

*The hilltop hour would not be half
so wonderful if there were no
dark valleys to traverse.*
HELEN KELLER

Peace

You, LORD, give true peace to those who depend on you, because they trust you.
ISAIAH 26:3 NCV

Peace is to the kingdom of God what oxygen is to the atmosphere. Considering this truth, you may be wondering why you so often feel agitated and anxious. Think of it this way: though oxygen permeates the air around us, we must breathe it into our lungs for it to do us any good. You must choose to let God rule in your heart. You must invite Him in. As you open your heart to Him, the peace will follow.

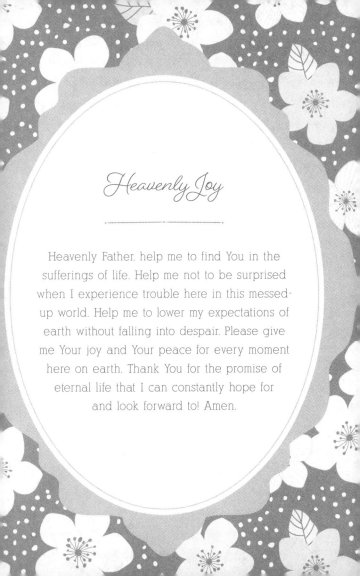

Heavenly Joy

Heavenly Father, help me to find You in the
sufferings of life. Help me not to be surprised
when I experience trouble here in this messed-
up world. Help me to lower my expectations of
earth without falling into despair. Please give
me Your joy and Your peace for every moment
here on earth. Thank You for the promise of
eternal life that I can constantly hope for
and look forward to! Amen.

I urge, then, first of all, that petitions, prayers, intercession and thanksgiving be made for all people—for kings and all those in authority, that we may live peaceful and quiet lives in all godliness and holiness. This is good, and pleases God our Savior, who wants all people to be saved and to come to a knowledge of the truth.
1 Timothy 2:1-4 niv

For the despondent, every day brings trouble; for the happy heart, life is a continual feast.
Proverbs 15:15 nlt

POWER IN
PRAYER

Aligned with God

I also pray that you will understand the incredible greatness of God's power for us who believe him. This is the same mighty power that raised Christ from the dead and seated him in the place of honor at God's right hand in the heavenly realms.

EPHESIANS 1:19–20 NLT

In the book *The Prayer Factor* by evangelist Sammy Tippit, you'll find this thought-provoking idea: it's men and women shining their lights for Christ who attract the world. In fact, Tippit calls prayer the "branding iron" of God. He says that time on our knees brings victory to life. Are you experiencing victory? Do you have the mark of God on you?

Prayer is powerful and is also a great mystery. We cannot see the spiritual realm, but God's Word tells us that our prayers are powerful and effective—something indeed happens when we pray. (Read Revelation 8 to see one of the amazing things that happens when we pray!)

Prayer aligns our hearts with the heart of God. We do not pray just to send our greatest wishes up to the sky. When we pray God's will, God changes us. And as He changes us, those around us take notice. They see a life in tune with God. They see *life*—not religion. So not only do our prayers change us, but they can change those around us who are watching.

In my distress I prayed to the LORD,
and the LORD answered me and set me
free. The LORD is for me, so I will have no
fear. What can mere people do to me?
PSALM 118:5-6 NLT

Devote yourselves to prayer
with an alert mind and a thankful heart.
COLOSSIANS 4:2 NLT

"If you abide in me, and my words abide
in you, ask whatever you wish,
and it will be done for you."
JOHN 15:7 ESV

God keeps his distance from the wicked;
he closely attends to the prayers
of God-loyal people.
PROVERBS 15:29 MSG

*More things are wrought by prayer
than this world dreams of.*
ALFRED LORD TENNYSON

---

*When the devil sees a man or woman who
really believes in prayer, who knows how to
pray, and who really does pray, and, above
all, when he sees a whole church on its face
before God in prayer, he trembles as much
as he ever did, for he knows that his day in
that church or community is at an end.*
R. A. TORREY

Prayer

Pray and ask God for everything you need,
always giving thanks.
PHILIPPIANS 4:6 NCV

Prayer is quite simply conversation with God. What a joyous privilege we have to be able to speak to Him—Almighty God—whenever we desire. How could you ever get enough of those times with Him? Meet with Him often to talk about your life. Tell Him your troubles and leave your worries at His feet. Confess your sins to Him and receive His forgiveness. Tell Him how much you love Him and how grateful you are to be His daughter. He is always ready to listen.

Confidence in Prayer

Heavenly Father, allow me to believe the truth
that You delight in me and want to be my
friend! Because of what Jesus did for me on
the cross, I can come to You with confidence.
God, that is so amazing to me! Thank You! Help
me to step out in faith believing that Your
power—the same power that raised Christ
from the grave—is available to me on a
constant basis. Let me live that I may
praise You (Psalm 119:175)! Amen.

"With a God like this loving you, you can pray very simply. Like this: Our Father in heaven, reveal who you are. Set the world right; do what's best—as above, so below. Keep us alive with three square meals. Keep us forgiven with you and forgiving others. Keep us safe from ourselves and the Devil. You're in charge! You can do anything you want! You're ablaze in beauty! Yes. Yes. Yes."

MATTHEW 6:13 MSG

We must begin to believe that God, in the
mystery of prayer, has entrusted us with a
force that can move the Heavenly world, and
can bring its power down to earth.
ANDREW MURRAY

On his knees, the believer is invincible.
CHARLES SPURGEON

Life without hope is an empty, boring,
and useless life. I cannot imagine that
I could strive for something if I did not
carry hope in me. I am thankful to God
for this gift. It is as big as life itself.
VACLAV HAVEL

Power and Success

*[It is not that] we think we can do anything
of lasting value by ourselves. Our only power
and success comes from God.*
2 CORINTHIANS 3:5 TLB

God created you for success, but He never planned for
you to acquire it alone. You may experience a small
measure of success here and there by your own wit,
but imagine where you can go in God. True success
comes when you are willing to say, "It's not about me
but all about You, Lord." Then He is free to take you to
a level that you can achieve only with His strength and
power propelling you. Then you will discover lasting
success in Him.

Alive in Me

Living God, allow me never to forget Your truths, Your purposes, and Your great power alive in me! Give me the desire to come to You first, before anyone or anything else. You care deeply about all of my decisions. And as I live in Your freedom, remind me of Your presence. Amen.

*Therefore, confess your sins to one another
and pray for one another, that you may
be healed. The prayer of a righteous
person has great power as it is working.*
JAMES 5:16 ESV

---

*And this is the confidence that we have toward
him, that if we ask anything according to his
will he hears us. And if we know that he hears
us in whatever we ask, we know that we have
the requests that we have asked of him.*
1 JOHN 5:14–15 ESV

---

*The Spirit of God, who raised Jesus from
the dead, lives in you. And just as God raised
Christ Jesus from the dead, he will give life
to your mortal bodies by this same
Spirit living within you.*
ROMANS 8:11 NLT

HAPPINESS
AND JOY

A Balm for the Soul

May the God of hope fill you with all
joy and peace as you trust in him,
so that you may overflow with hope
by the power of the Holy Spirit.

ROMANS 15:13 NIV

Consider the following passage:

> The LORD is compassionate and gracious, slow
> to anger, abounding in love. He will not always
> accuse, nor will he harbor his anger forever; he
> does not treat us as our sins deserve or repay
> us according to our iniquities. For as high as the
> heavens are above the earth, so great is his love
> for those who fear him; as far as the east is from
> the west, so far has he removed our transgres-
> sions from us. As a father has compassion on his
> children, so the LORD has compassion on those
> who fear him. PSALM 103:8–13 NIV

This psalm is a balm to the hardened soul. God doesn't treat us as our sins deserve. He is compassionate. He is gracious. Because of Jesus' work on the cross, God is not angry with us! Instead, He is abounding in love. He sees us as Jesus sees us: *paid for!* Our sins have been obliterated.

Theologian J. I. Packer said, "There is. . .equally great incentive to worship and love God in the thought that, for some unfathomable reason, He wants me as His friend, and desires to be my friend, and has given His Son to die for me in order to realize this purpose."

Our joy and happiness come from knowing and walking in that truth!

For you make me glad by your deeds, LORD;
I sing for joy at what your hands have done.
PSALM 92:4 NIV

Satisfy us in the morning with your unfailing
love, that we may sing for joy and
be glad all our days.
PSALM 90:14 NIV

Yes, joyful are those who live like this!
Joyful indeed are those whose
God is the LORD.
PSALM 144:15 NLT

The LORD is my strength and shield.
I trust him with all my heart. He helps me,
and my heart is filled with joy. I burst
out in songs of thanksgiving.
PSALM 28:7 NLT

*It is not how much we have, but how
much we enjoy, that makes happiness.*

CHARLES SPURGEON

*It is pleasing to the dear God whenever you
rejoice or laugh from the bottom of your heart.*

MARTIN LUTHER

*Thou art giving and forgiving,
ever blessing, ever blessed,
Wellspring of the joy of living,
ocean depth of happy rest!*

HENRY J. VAN DYKE

Rejoice!

May the righteous be glad and rejoice before
God; may they be happy and joyful.
PSALM 68:3 NIV

Many women believe that happiness is a result of success. "When I find the right person to marry, I'll be happy." "When I achieve my career goals. . ." "When I can afford the home I really want. . ." The truth is that real happiness—deep inner joy—is the result of living in right relationship with God rather than the trappings of success. Regardless of what you may be facing—good and bad—be happy knowing you are pleasing your heavenly Father.

Seeing Your Goodness

Father I trust that I will see Your goodness
here and now as I go through life on earth.
My greatest joy is knowing You and living for
You. You have forgiven me so much—help me
to love much. You have removed the weight of
sin and stress from my shoulders and have
allowed me to dance. You have removed my
sins as far as the east is from the west.
You have given me freedom and a clear
conscience. Thank You, Jesus! Fill me
with joy in Your presence all
the days of my life. Amen.

*Take delight in the Lord, and he will give you
your heart's desires. Commit everything you
do to the Lord. Trust him, and he will help
you. He will make your innocence radiate
like the dawn, and the justice of your
cause will shine like the noonday sun.*
PSALM 37:4-6 NLT

*But let all who take refuge in you be glad;
let them ever sing for joy. Spread your
protection over them, that those who love
your name may rejoice in you. Surely,
Lord, you bless the righteous; you surround
them with your favor as with a shield.*
PSALM 5:11-12 NIV

*Abandon yourself utterly for the love of God,
and in this way you will become truly happy.*
HENRY SUSO

---

*If we learn how to give of ourselves,
to forgive others, and to live with thanksgiving,
we need not seek happiness. It will seek us.*
UNKNOWN

---

*If anyone would tell you the shortest, surest
way to happiness and all perfection, he must
tell you to make it a rule to thank and praise
God for everything that happens to you.*
WILLIAM LAW

The Joy of Blessings

Grace and peace be yours in abundance.
1 Peter 1:2 NIV

As you look around at God's blessings in your life, close your eyes and look inward, as well. God has also provided you with an abundance of grace and peace. Grace that allows you to be who you genuinely are and the peace of knowing that who you are is just fine with Him. Women are wonderfully emotional people. . . . If your inner places are full of joy, praise Him! If your inner places are dark and empty, invite God to fill them to overflowing with His goodness.

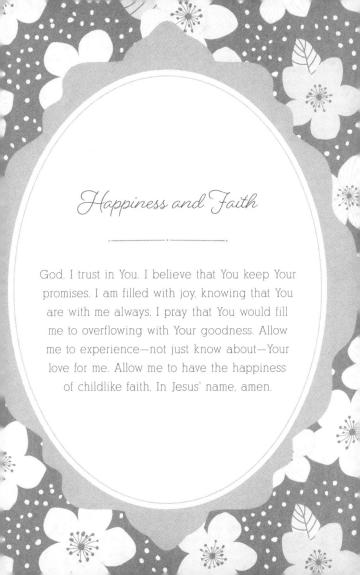

Happiness and Faith

God, I trust in You. I believe that You keep Your
promises. I am filled with joy, knowing that You
are with me always. I pray that You would fill
me to overflowing with Your goodness. Allow
me to experience—not just know about—Your
love for me. Allow me to have the happiness
of childlike faith. In Jesus' name, amen.

Don't put your confidence in powerful people;
there is no help for you there. When they
breathe their last, they return to the earth,
and all their plans die with them. But joyful
are those who have the God of Israel as
their helper, whose hope is in the LORD their
God. He made heaven and earth, the sea,
and everything in them. He keeps
every promise forever.
PSALM 146:3-6 NLT

REST AND
RENEWAL

Rest of Heart

"Only in returning to me and resting in
me will you be saved. In quietness and
confidence is your strength."

ISAIAH 30:15 NLT

Rest is a very good and needed thing. If you go to bed each night wishing there were more hours in a day, then you are doing more than God intended. You need to come to Him and rest. Realign your heart with God's. Ask Him to show you His will and His daily plans for you. They often look much, much different than what we have planned for ourselves. God wants you to return to Him for counsel, for friendship, for the building of your faith—for rest. He might be asking you to cut out a lot of good things in your life. He might be asking you to say no to some good things so that you can say yes to better things He has for you. As you come to Him for rest, He will give you the confidence and strength to do what He is asking of you. You will be able to trust the wisdom of doing things God's way instead of your way.

Hannah Whitall Smith said, "Seeing our Father in everything makes life one long thanksgiving and gives a rest of heart." As we look for God, we find Him in new ways. We can be thankful and hopeful in difficult times because God is with us, giving us rest of heart each day.

"Be still, and know that I am God.
I will be exalted among the nations,
I will be exalted in the earth!"
PSALM 46:10 ESV

Be still before the LORD
and wait patiently for him.
PSALM 37:7 NIV

Then Jesus said, "Let's go off by ourselves
to a quiet place and rest awhile."
MARK 6:31 NLT

"For I will satisfy the weary soul,
and every languishing soul I will replenish."
JEREMIAH 31:25 ESV

*Thou hast made us for Thyself, O Lord,
and our heart is restless until
it finds its rest in Thee.*

AUGUSTINE

---

*When outward strength is broken, faith rests
on the promises. In the midst of sorrow,
faith draws the sting out of every trouble
and takes out the bitterness
from every affliction.*

RICHARD CECIL

Strengthened and Renewed

I can do everything through Christ,
who gives me strength.
PHILIPPIANS 4:13 NLT

You're probably busier than you've ever been—doing more than you've ever done. Maybe you feel exhausted—physically, mentally, and emotionally. God has given you strength for your days, even the toughest ones. He is the source you can draw on when you feel your supply is running low. You don't have to go at life alone. When you reach for Him, He's always there, ready to refresh you. Find quiet moments to dip your soul into His supply. You'll come away strengthened and renewed.

I Rest in Your Truth

Heavenly Father, thank You for Your many
blessings and Your unfailing love! Allow me
to rest in the truth that You are forever the
same. In times of blessing and in hard
times, too, bring me reminders of
Your faithfulness and love. Amen.

"Come to me, all who labor and are heavy
laden, and I will give you rest. Take my yoke
upon you, and learn from me, for I am gentle
and lowly in heart, and you will find rest for
your souls. For my yoke is easy,
and my burden is light."
MATTHEW 11:28-30 ESV

It's useless to rise early and go to bed late,
and work your worried fingers to
the bone. Don't you know he enjoys
giving rest to those he loves?
PSALM 127:2 MSG

[God] knows everything about us.
And He cares about everything. Moreover,
He can manage every situation. And He
loves us! Surely this is enough to open
the wellsprings of joy. . . . And joy is
always a source of strength.
HANNAH WHITALL SMITH

Burdens

*"Come to me, all you who are weary
and burdened, and I will give you rest."*
MATTHEW 11:28 NIV

Weary. Burdened. Need rest. Those words read like a repeating entry in a woman's daily journal. Most women feel they have earned the right to be burdened. What else but weary could they be with all they have to do? Jesus said that He would give rest to those who are weary. He would lighten our loads. Take one burden at a time and hand it over to Him. And then rest in the peace that Jesus has our lives in the palm of His hand.

Stress Less

Heavenly Father, in the midst of the chaos and
messes of my life, I need the peace that only
You offer. I come to You to find rest and renewal.
Increase my faith in You. Help me to trust You no
matter what kind of trouble comes knocking at
my door. I know I worry unnecessarily,
for You have always been faithful in the
past. None of these issues surprise You.
Help me to trust You more and
stress less. Amen.

The Lord is a refuge for the oppressed, a stronghold in times of trouble. Those who know your name trust in you, for you, Lord, have never forsaken those who seek you.
Psalm 9:9-10 niv

But you are a tower of refuge to the poor, O Lord, a tower of refuge to the needy in distress. You are a refuge from the storm and a shelter from the heat. For the oppressive acts of ruthless people are like a storm beating against a wall.
Isaiah 25:4 nlt

And he said, "My presence will go with you, and I will give you rest."
Exodus 33:14 esv

PROTECTION
AND TRUST

The Great Protector

---

*But let all who take refuge in you rejoice;
let them sing joyful praises forever. Spread
your protection over them, that all who
love your name may be filled with joy.*

PSALM 5:11 NLT

God is our great protector. God's protection probably looks way different than what we wish it did at times. People still have accidents. Pain still visits us. We don't live a fairy-tale life. Does that mean God isn't protecting us? No. God's healing presence is always with us when we go through pain. God wants to heal our souls, which are eternal, even when our bodies are in pain.

So how does God protect us?

God protects us from ourselves. Theologian J. I. Packer said, "Your faith will not fail while God sustains it; you are not strong enough to fall away while God is resolved to hold you." As a child of God, you are deeply loved and held in His arms. If you have committed your life to Christ, He will not let go of you. He will never leave you. Even if you try to run and hide, He is there (see Psalm 139).

God protects us from evil. The name of Jesus has great power. Someday every knee will bow and tongue confess that Jesus Christ is Lord (Philippians 2:9-11). When you are crippled with fear, overwhelmed with worry, or feeling oppressed by the enemy, speak the name of Jesus out loud and trust in His power! Remember, He protects you and will not abandon you.

As we love God and sing His praises, we are protected and filled with joy!

But the Lord is faithful, and he will strengthen
you and protect you from the evil one.
2 THESSALONIANS 3:3 NIV

We know that God's children do not make a
practice of sinning, for God's Son holds them
securely, and the evil one cannot touch them.
1 JOHN 5:18 NLT

No test or temptation that comes your way is
beyond the course of what others have had
to face. All you need to remember is that God
will never let you down; he'll never let you
be pushed past your limit; he'll always
be there to help you come through it.
1 CORINTHIANS 10:13 MSG

He who trusts in the Lord has a diploma for wisdom granted by inspiration: happy is he now, and happier shall he be above. Lord, teach me the wisdom of faith. Faith is the radar that sees through the fog the reality of things at a distance that the human eye cannot see.

CORRIE TEN BOOM

God will not permit any troubles to come upon us unless He has a specific plan by which great blessing can come out of the difficulty.

PETER MARSHALL

Protection

The LORD your God will lead you
and protect you on every side.
ISAIAH 52:12 GNT

We all have fears—fear of harm, fear of losing a child, fear of being alone, fear of failure. When your fears rise up and threaten to overcome you, when you feel sick in the pit of your stomach and your heart aches with anxiety, remember this: God is with you every day, every hour, every moment. Focus on Him, really focus, and you will see that your fears are nothing more than speculation that is swept away in His presence.

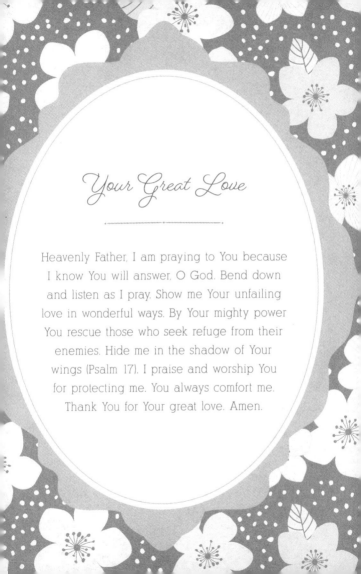

Your Great Love

Heavenly Father, I am praying to You because I know You will answer, O God. Bend down and listen as I pray. Show me Your unfailing love in wonderful ways. By Your mighty power You rescue those who seek refuge from their enemies. Hide me in the shadow of Your wings (Psalm 17). I praise and worship You for protecting me. You always comfort me. Thank You for Your great love. Amen.

"So be strong and courageous! Do not be afraid and do not panic before them. For the Lord *your God will personally go ahead of you. He will neither fail you nor abandon you."*

Deuteronomy 31:6 nlt

―――――――・―――――――

"So do not fear, for I am with you; do not be dismayed, for I am your God. I will strengthen you and help you; I will uphold you with my righteous right hand."

Isaiah 41:10 niv

―――――――・―――――――

The righteous person faces many troubles, but the Lord *comes to the rescue each time.*

Psalm 34:19 nlt

God came to us because God wanted
to join us on the road, to listen to our story,
and to help us realize that we are not
walking in circles but moving toward
the house of peace and joy.

THOMAS MERTON

There will be peace and tranquility in the
Christian heart; but only as long as our
faith is watchful; if, however, our faith
sleeps, we are in danger.

AUGUSTINE

Either we trust in God, and in that case we
neither trust in ourselves, nor in our fellow-
men, nor in circumstances, nor in anything
besides; or we do trust in one or more of
these, and in that case do not trust in God.

GEORGE MÜLLER

No Reason to Fear

The LORD watches over all who love him.
PSALM 145:20 NIV

Like any loving parent, your heavenly Father keeps you in His constant care, never letting you out of His sight. You have no reason to fear, for He is always with you, ready to face whatever comes your way. He will not fail you. In some cases, He will warn you ahead of time. In others, He will supernaturally remove you from a dangerous situation. And there will be times when He will hold your hand as you walk through fire. He is your God!

Protection and Favor

Father God, when I am afraid, I will put my
trust in You. When I don't understand, I will put
my trust in You. When I just don't feel like it, I
will put my trust in You. Let these words be true
in my life; not just lip service, but a total heart
transformation. I ask for Your protection and
favor as I follow after You. Be near me, Lord
Jesus. Help me to remember Your promise
that You will never leave me. Amen.

The Lord is my light and my salvation—
so why should I be afraid? The Lord is
my fortress, protecting me from
danger, so why should I tremble?
PSALM 27:1 NLT

"Blessed are those who trust in the
Lord and have made the Lord their
hope and confidence."
JEREMIAH 17:7 NLT

Though I am surrounded by troubles, you will
protect me from the anger of my enemies.
You reach out your hand, and the power
of your right hand saves me. The Lord will
work out his plans for my life—for your
faithful love, O Lord, endures forever.
Don't abandon me, for you made me.
PSALM 138:7-8 NLT

FAITH AND
PROVISION

Share Your Heart

———— • ————

*"But if you can do anything,
take pity on us and help us."
"'If you can'?" said Jesus. "Everything is
possible for one who believes."
Immediately the boy's father
exclaimed, "I do believe; help me
overcome my unbelief!"*
MARK 9:22-24 NIV

A man brought Jesus a boy who was possessed by a demon. The boy's father had his doubts that Jesus could really heal his son who had been ill most of his life. Jesus reminded him that with faith everything is possible. We must admit that we have moments like this boy's father. We have trouble believing that God can actually handle our problems. We think He needs our help, so we manipulate circumstances and forget God so that we can have the outcome we desire. We carry the burden alone instead of trusting that the God of the universe wants to help with our problems.

When you find yourself in that situation, take your thoughts captive to Christ and pause before you do something you will later regret. Tell God your heart. He is big enough to handle your honesty. Ask Him to help you overcome your unbelief and to give you the gift of faith (see Ephesians 2:8-9).

Hebrews 11 gives us more insight into the life of faith. Verse 6 tells us that "without faith it is impossible to please God, because anyone who comes to him must believe that he exists and that he rewards those who earnestly seek him" (NIV). God rewards our faith as we come to Him with all of our thoughts, problems, and ideas.

Great is Thy faithfulness!
Great is Thy faithfulness!
Morning by morning new mercies I see.
All I have needed Thy hand hath provided.
Great is Thy faithfulness, Lord, unto me!

THOMAS O. CHISHOLM

Grace is no stationary thing; it is ever
becoming. It is flowing straight out of God's
heart. Grace does nothing but re-form
and convey God. . . . God, the ground
of the soul, and grace go together.

MEISTER ECKHART

If the Lord be with us, we have no cause
of fear. His eye is upon us, His arm over us,
His ear open to our prayer—His grace
sufficient, His promise unchangeable.

JOHN NEWTON

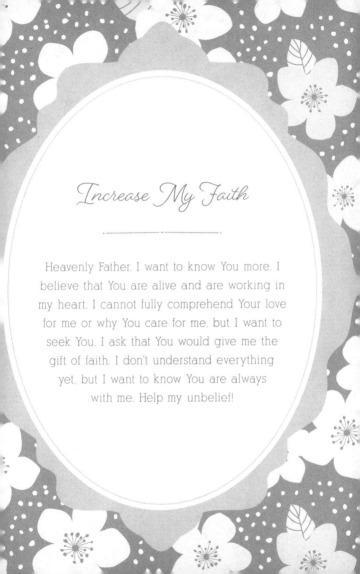

Increase My Faith

Heavenly Father, I want to know You more. I believe that You are alive and are working in my heart. I cannot fully comprehend Your love for me or why You care for me, but I want to seek You. I ask that You would give me the gift of faith. I don't understand everything yet, but I want to know You are always with me. Help my unbelief!

*And God will generously provide all you
need. Then you will always have
everything you need and plenty
left over to share with others.*
2 Corinthians 9:8 NLT

*The faithful love of the Lord never ends!
His mercies never cease. Great is his
faithfulness; his mercies begin
afresh each morning.*
Lamentations 3:22-23 NLT

*So the Word became human and made his
home among us. He was full of unfailing
love and faithfulness. And we have seen
his glory, the glory of the Father's
one and only Son.*
John 1:14 NLT

What a serene and quiet life might you lead
if you would leave providing to the God of
providence! With a little oil in the cruse, and
a handful of meal in the barrel, Elijah outlived
the famine, and you will do the same. If God
cares for you, why need you care too? Can
you trust Him for your soul and not for your
body? He has never refused to bear your
burdens, He has never fainted under their
weight. Come, then, soul! have done with fretful
care, and leave all thy concerns in the
hand of a gracious God.

CHARLES SPURGEON

God Provides

"Your Father knows what you need before you ask him."
MATTHEW 6:8 NIV

God wants you to have everything you need for a great life. But sometimes you pray and things don't happen when you expect them to. You must trust that His timing is perfect. None of us live in a vacuum. Sometimes your request requires compliance on the part of other people, and they may not be prompt to respond. Don't give up. God will answer your prayer in the perfect way at the perfect time.

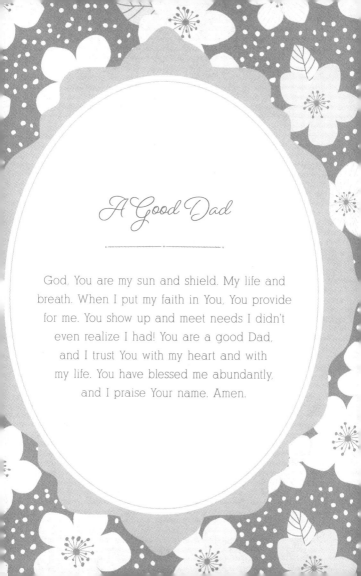

A Good Dad

God, You are my sun and shield. My life and
breath. When I put my faith in You, You provide
for me. You show up and meet needs I didn't
even realize I had! You are a good Dad,
and I trust You with my heart and with
my life. You have blessed me abundantly,
and I praise Your name. Amen.

For the L<small>ORD</small> God is our sun and our shield.
He gives us grace and glory. The L<small>ORD</small>
will withhold no good thing from
those who do what is right.
P<small>SALM</small> 84:11 <small>NLT</small>